Learn to Sew: Kids

My First
Sewing Machine

FASHION SCHOOL

Alison McNicol

Learn to sew and make *cool* clothes!

A Kyle Craig Publication

www.kyle-craig.com

First published in 2012 by Kyle Craig Publishing

Text and illustration copyright © 2012 Alison McNicol

Design and illustration: Julie Anson

CRAFTS & HOBBIES/Crafts For Children
CRAFTS & HOBBIES/Sewing

ISBN 978-1-908707-05-5

Contents

Alison and some stitching friends

Hey there!

I'll never forget my first ever sewing machine, which I received for Christmas when I was just 8. It started my love of sewing and I had so much fun making all sorts of things — toys, cool things for my room, clothes, bags and gifts. Now I just LOVE helping others to learn how to sew!

If you already have my other *My First Sewing Machine Book* then you may already be using your machine — if not, don't worry as this book revisits all the skills you'll need to get confident using your machine, and adds LOTS more that you'll need to get started creating your very own cool fashions!

Using a sewing machine is easy once you know how! Just take your time to learn all about your machine and what each part does, and always pay close attention when you're using your machine to make sure you are sewing safely.

Once you've mastered using your machine there will be no stopping you!

Are you ready? Let's SEW!

Alison McNicol

Sewing kit essentials

It's a good idea to get yourself a good sewing box to keep your kit all in one place. This could be anything from a classic wooden workbox, to a fancy sewing box or even an old cookie tin. The items listed here are the basic items you should need to get going. Once you get the sewing bug there are all sorts of other bits and bobs you can add to your collection!

Dressmakers Chalk: This is also called *tailors chalk* and comes in different shapes, such as pencils, triangles or circles. It's is used for drawing lines on fabrics. Use white chalk for dark fabrics and coloured chalk for light or patterned fabrics.

Needles: It's handy to have a few different sized hand sewing needles. A medium size needle will do for most jobs, but a tough fabric like denim will need a thicker needle. A needle with a big 'eye' is needed for thicker thread or embroidery thread.

Pins: Dressmaking pins can come as basic steel pins or with a variety of colourful heads. A pincushion is also handy for storing pins while you work.

Scissors: It's a good idea to have a few pairs for different purposes:
Dressmaking scissors: have long, sharp steel blades and are for cutting out fabric pieces.
Paper scissors: useful for cutting out paper patterns so you do not blunt your dressmaking scissors.
Pinking Shears: cut a zig zag edge which can stop fabric from fraying.

Sewing scissors: smaller than dressmaking scissors and are handy for trimming seams or threads.

Seam Ripper: This is also called an *unpicker*. It has a sharp little hook that helps you to easily rip out seams or tacking. Very handy if you make a mistake on the sewing machine!

Sewing Machine Needles: The needlesize and type is determined by the fabric you are using. The needles your machine comes with will be fine for most standard fabrics or cottons. For other fabrics, such as denim, silk or stretchy fabrics you will need to use special needles that are the correct size for the fabric.

Tape Measure: A tape measure is essential for measuring fabrics and taking measurements. But you can also use a ruler or solid measuring stick.

Fabrics & threads

The choice of fabric is important when planning a project. As well as looking at the colour and pattern of a fabric, think about how it will look as the finished item. Is it heavy enough for the purpose, will it hang well when sewn and not crease too much?

There are so many cool fabrics available, and it's great to start a collection so you will always have some fabric to hand whenever you feel like making something!

Fabrics

Calico: is a plain natural coloured woven cotton that has a gorgeous old fashioned feel to it and comes in a variety of widths.

Cotton: one of the most versatile and popular fabrics, cotton is a natural fabric made from the hairs that cover the seed pod of the cotton plant. Available in a variety of light to medium weights.

Man made fabrics: these include polyester, nylon and rayon. Some of these are slippery and crease easily, while others likepolyester are very crease-resistant. You can also get a mix of man-made and natural fabrics, like poly cotton, that combines the best qualities of both fabrics.

Threads

Cotton Thread: cotton thread is a fine, mercerised thread that is used for hand and machine stitching, usually on natural fabrics such as cotton, linen and woollen fabric.

Polyester Thread: this is a popular multi-purpose type of thread that can be used on all types of fabrics, for hand and machine stitching, and comes in a wide range of colours.

Silk Thread: this is a fine, yet strong thread that can be used for both hand and machine stitching. It is commonly used on silk and wool fabrics, and for hand-stitched buttonholes on finer fabrics.

How to use...
Fabric

So that we can follow **PROJECTS** cards and **PATTERNS**, it's important to know what all the words mean. With fabric, we talk about the **right** side and the **wrong** side of the fabric.

STEP 1

The *right side*, is the nice side, the one you want to be seen.

The *wrong side* is the back of the fabric or the nasty side. With patterned fabric it's usually quite easy to see which side is which.

STEP 2

If we're sewing something with straight or blanket stitch that we want to be seen, we may be told to place the *wrong sides* together. We then sew our stitches where needed.

STEP 3

If we're sewing something where we don't want the stitches to be seen — like a pillow or clothes — we may be told to put the *right sides* together before sewing.

STEP 4

Now when we turn it inside out — the *right side* is on the *outside*! See?

How to use...
A sewing machine

SEW…now you're ready to use a sewing machine?!

Learning to use a sewing machine is a bit like learning to drive a car or fly an aeroplane — we must learn how it all works first before we can use it **SAFELY**!

FIRST we're going to learn what all the **parts are called**, and what they **do**. We'll also learn some important things about sewing machine **safety** too.

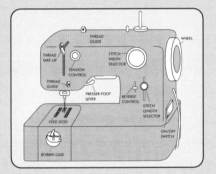

THEN, we're going to learn how to **thread** our machines properly. Without thread, we wouldn't be able to make any stitches!

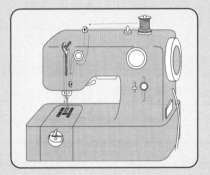

NEXT we'll see how to how to **control** our fabric as it passes through the machine so we make stitches exactly where we want them.

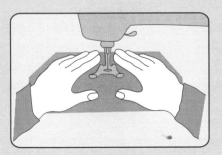

LASTLY we'll practice using the machine to sew **straight lines**, **curves** and **turn corners**.

They say Practice Makes Perfect, and that's very true. The more that you practice, the more you can do! Get to know your machine, each and every part, and in no time at all you'll be ready to start ....SEWING !!

Parts of a sewing machine

Each sewing machine will come with it's own instruction booklet...but most machines have very similar parts. Why not compare this picture to YOUR sewing machine. Try to find each part on yours!

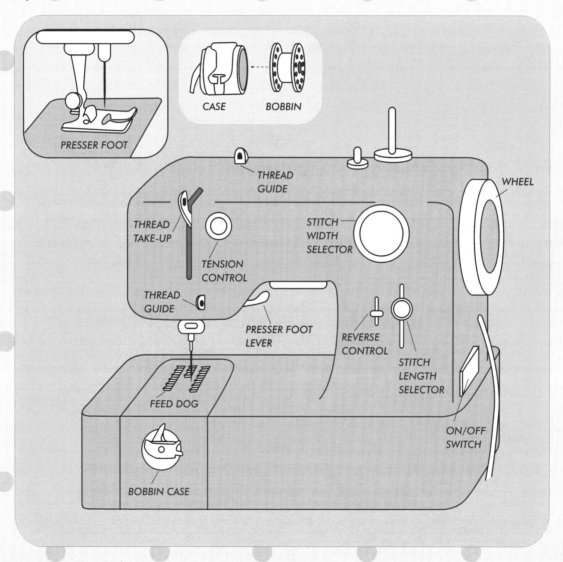

PRESSER FOOT

CASE   BOBBIN

THREAD GUIDE

WHEEL

THREAD TAKE-UP

STITCH WIDTH SELECTOR

TENSION CONTROL

THREAD GUIDE

PRESSER FOOT LEVER

REVERSE CONTROL

STITCH LENGTH SELECTOR

ON/OFF SWITCH

FEED DOG

BOBBIN CASE

WHEEL	This turns as the machine goes. By turning the wheel *towards* you, you can raise and lower the needle to place it exactly where you want.
ON/OFF SWITCH	This turns the power on and off.
REVERSE CONTROL	Use this lever to sew backwards.
STITCH WIDTH SELECTOR	Adjust this dial to change your straight stitch to a zigzag stitch.
STITCH LENGTH SELECTOR	Adjust this to set the length of your stitch.
TENSION CONTROL	This controls the amount of pressure on your thread as it passes through your machine. You shouldn't normally have to adjust this.
THREAD GUIDES	These guides lead your thread from the spool all the way to the needle.
THREAD TAKE-UP	This lever helps to keep the tension on the thread. We can also look at this to see if our needle is *up* or *down* when we want to stop or start.
BOBBIN CASE	The bobbin case holds the bobbin, and the bobbin holds the bottom thread.
PRESSER FOOT	The presser foot works with the feed dog to hold the fabric and move it through the machine. Presser feet come in different shapes for different jobs.
PRESSER FOOT LEVER	This lever raises and lowers the presser foot. Raise it to insert your fabric. Lower it when ready to sew.
FEED DOG	The feed dog teeth and presser foot work together to move the fabric along. Can you see the teeth?

How to...
Thread your machine

Check the instruction booklet to see where all the thread guides are on your machine.

Follow the path from the spool, through all the thread guides to the needle's eye. Don't miss any out!

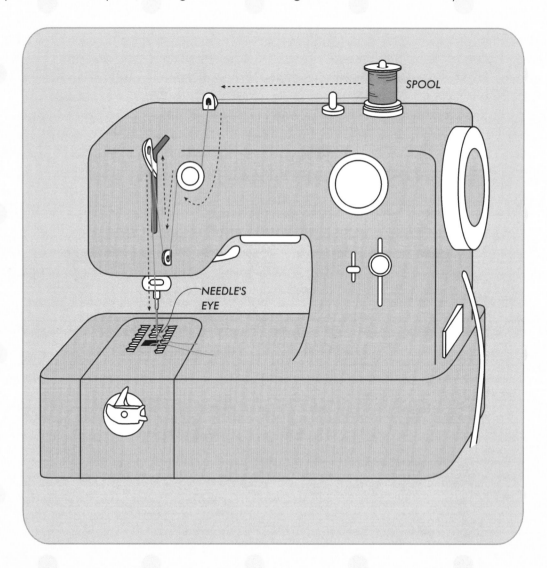

SPOOL

NEEDLE'S EYE

How to...
Fill the bobbin

Sewing machines use two different threads — the top spool and the bottom bobbin. When the machine goes, both threads join together to make a stitch!

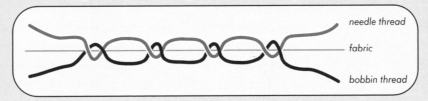

STEP 1
Follow the thread guides from the spool to the bobbin winder and wind thread onto your bobbin.

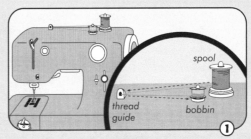

STEP 2
Put the bobbin in the bobbin case...

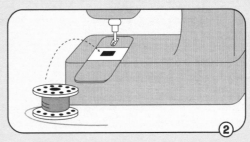

STEP 3
...and then turn the wheel to bring the bobbin thread up through the needle hole.

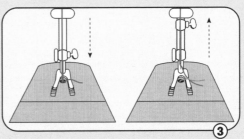

Hands and positioning

It's important that we're sitting comfortably at our sewing machine. Make sure that you can sit up straight with your feet flat on the floor. Can you reach the foot pedal easily?

Make a triangle with your hands, resting your fingertips on the fabric to lightly guide it through. Practice controlling your fabric so that the machine sews exactly where you want it to!

Don't PUSH or PULL the fabric ...just GUIDE it!

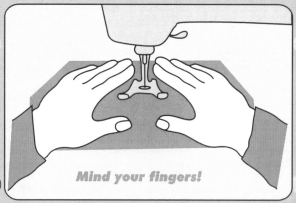

Mind your fingers!

Quiz: Parts of a sewing machine

Can you remember the names of all the parts of a sewing machine? Fill in the quiz below!

THREAD GUIDE   ON/OFF SWITCH   THREAD TAKE- UP   FEED DOG
WHEEL   BOBBIN CASE   TENSION CONTROL   PRESSER FOOT   STITCH WIDTH SELECTOR
STITCH LENGTH SELECTOR   PRESSER FOOT LIFTER   REVERSE CONTROL

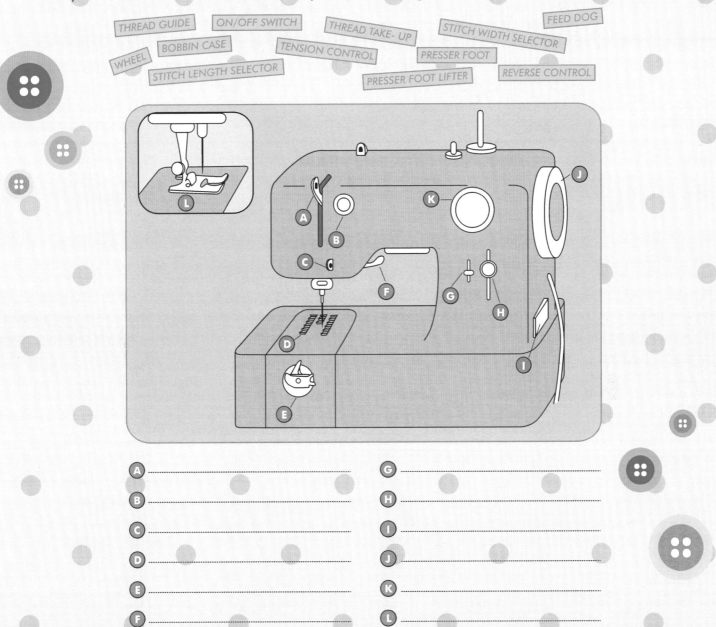

A ....
B ....
C ....
D ....
E ....
F ....
G ....
H ....
I ....
J ....
K ....
L ....

How to...
Turn corners

To turn corners, or 'pivot' with a sewing machine, we need to pay close attention to our needle and our presser foot. Imagine your needle is a ballerina's foot! The needle, like the dancer's toe, must stay down as you lift the presser foot, turn the fabric, then drop the presser foot back down.

STEP 1
Check the needle is down through the fabric. If not, turn the wheel towards you until it is.

STEP 2
Lift the presser foot using the lever.

STEP 3
Turn your fabric to the new direction.

PIVOT!

STEP 4
Put your presser foot back down before you start sewing again in the new direction. Now let's practice turning corners...!

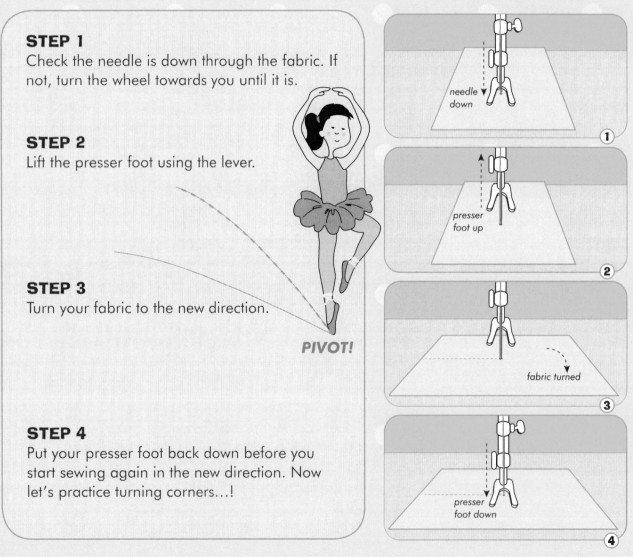

Practice...
Turning corners

Copy this page, don't tear the book!

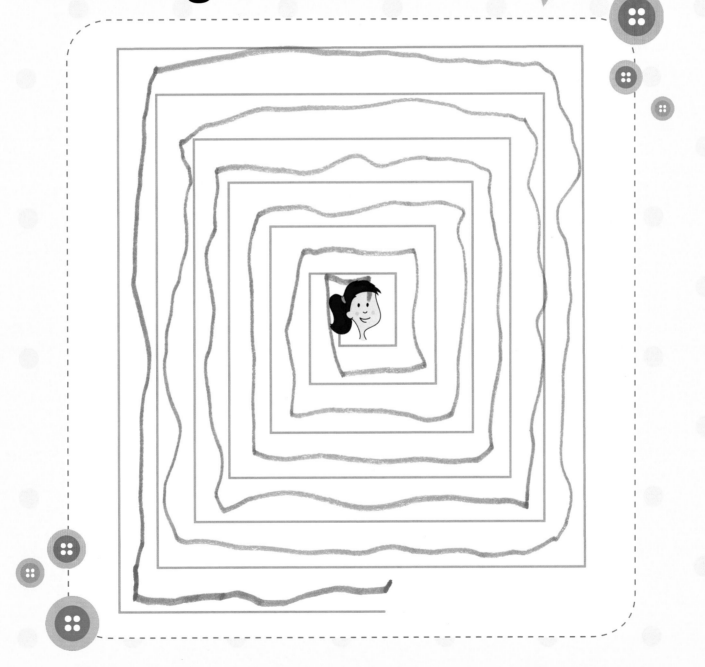

How to sew...
Lock stitches

When we sew by hand, we always **start** and **finish** with a **DOUBLE STITCH**. It's no different with a sewing machine — we do the same and this is called a **LOCK STITCH**.

STEP 1
Start sewing for a few stitches on your machine.

STEP 2
Use the **reverse** lever to stitch **backwards** to where you started.

STEP 3
Release the **reverse** lever and stitch on as normal.

STEP 4
Stitch all the way to where you need to end then **reverse** for a few stitches. See if you can practice doing lock stitches on your practice pages.

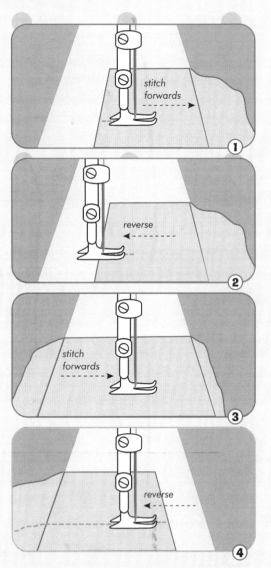

Practice sewing...
Lock stitches

Copy this page, don't tear the book!

Don't forget to start by going forwards for a few stitches, then reverse to make your lock stitch... the blue dots show you where!

Practice sewing...
A star shape

Copy this page, don't tear the book!

Remember to 'pivot' to change direction!

Practice sewing...
Curves

Copy this page, don't tear the book!

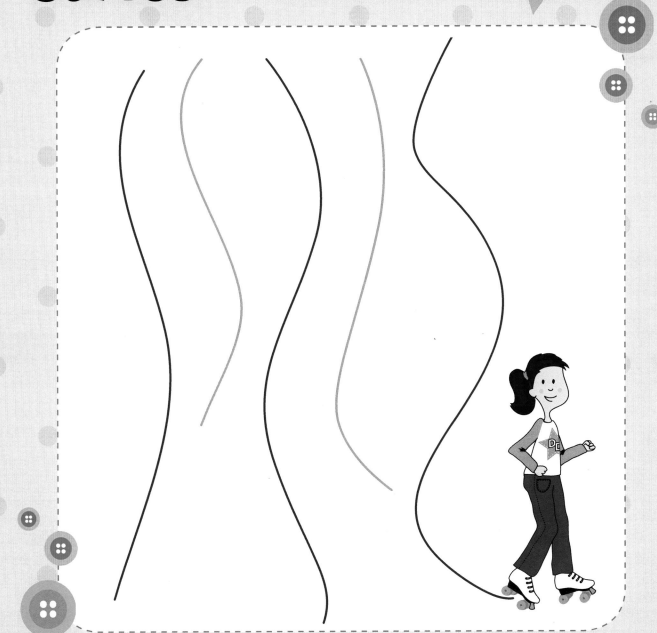

How to...
Sew a casing

A casing is like a big hem, or a tunnel, usually at the top of a bag or the waist of a skirt. We use the tunnel to thread through the cord or elastic before pulling it tight to make it gather.

STEP 1

First we need to sew a hem, to neaten the edge of the fabric. Placing your fabric WRONG side facing up, turn over the raw edge of the fabric towards you, by 1cm/¾ in. Iron in place, then pin and stitch.

STEP 2

Now that we have a neat edge, it's time to make the casing. Like before, turn the fabric towards you this time by 5cm/2in. Iron in place, then pin. Stitch a straight line, close to the bottom edge. Don't forget to begin and end with a LOCK STITCH!

STEP 3

To make it look even nicer we can also sew another straight line across the top, a bit down the folded edge. This will give us a lovely frill at the top!

STEP 4

Attach a big safety pin to each end of your cord or elastic and feed it through the tunnel until it comes out the other end! You can pin one end to your bag to stop it pulling through the tunnel! Now pull until it's as gathered as you need it, and tie the cord ends together.

Make sure you leave a big enough tunnel to feed your cord through!

How to...
Sew a hem

When we cut fabric it leaves a "raw" edge which could fray and doesn't look very good. A hem is a way of tidying up the edges of a fabric so they look nice. Look at your clothes, can you see the hems at the edges?

frayed hem

STEP 1

Fold the raw edge over, so that the wrong sides are touching. About 2cm/¾in. is usually plenty.

Make sure it's even all the way along, and pin. Make sure your pins are nearest the raw edge so they don't get in the way!

> Be careful to remove any pins if they're in the way!

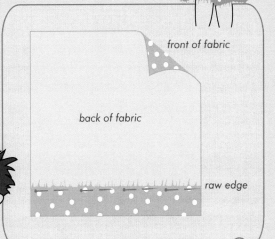

front of fabric

back of fabric

raw edge

①

STEP 2
Carefully iron in place and pin. Now sew a very straight line all along the hem.

STEP 3
Repeat — fold, iron, sew.

See how much nicer it looks now?

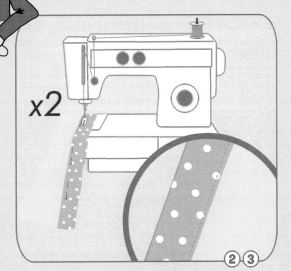

x2

② ③

Introduction to...
Sewing Patterns

Many beginners can be a bit scared at the prospect of choosing and using a sewing pattern, but by starting with a simple pattern and garment and getting used to the terminology and skills used, you will find you can quickly move on to any commercial sewing pattern you like! Here are some tips to help you unravel the mysteries that lay behind your sewing pattern.

Size: the best way to choose the correct size of sewing pattern is to take all the measurements of whomever you are making the garment for, write them down, and take these notes with you to the fabric store. Most sewing patterns actually fit a range of sizes, and you simply cut out the size you need.

Difficulty: most sewing patterns will note the degree of difficulty. If you have not sewn much before or have not used sewing patterns much, be sure to get one that is rated as easy. Slowly work your way up to more difficult projects.

Iron: take an iron on low heat and iron out your sewing pattern so that all of the pieces are nice and smooth.

Pre-read: just as with a recipe, it is a good idea to completely read through the pattern instruction sheet before you start working, rather than only reading it as you go. You can save yourself a lot of headaches by understanding the instructions before you start!

Pattern instruction sheet: this is a very important tool. It will tell you how to lay out your sewing pattern pieces and more. Look at the diagrams. Take note of special symbols.

My Measurements:

Chest ....

Waist...........................

Hip ....

Outside Leg...................

Skirt Length ....

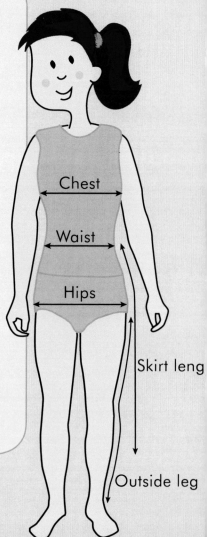

Chest

Waist

Hips

Skirt leng

Outside leg

Planning...
A Pattern

The instruction sheet that comes with your pattern has suggested layouts for pinning the pieces to the fabric. Make sure you understand the shadings on the layout that indicate which way to lay the right and wrong sides, linings, interfacings etc. Then lay out the fabric doubled with wrong sides together, unless instructed otherwise, and arrange the pieces on it as indicated. Make sure they all fit before you pin and cut.

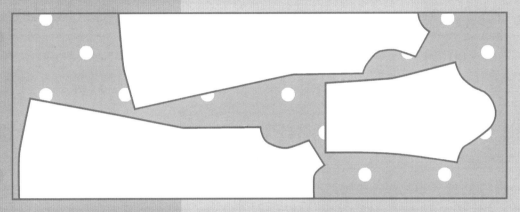

← →	**Grain Line**	Place on straight grain of fabric parallel to selvage (remember, the selvage is the the finished edge of the fabric that runs down both sides.)
	Fold Line	Place solid line on the fold of the fabric.
—·—·—·—	**Centre Line**	Centre marking of the front or back of garment.
	Notches and Dots	Locator marks for matching up points on fabric.
———	**Cutting Line**	Heavy solid line for cutting out the pattern and fabric.
═══	**Adjustment Line**	Double lines for lengthening or shortening the garment.
------	**Dart Line**	Short, broken lines indicate edges to be joined by stitching.

Make it! Wrap Skirt

Fabric Width: Measure around yourself — just above your hips, but below your waist (this is where your skirt will sit). Now double this measurement. This will be your fabric WIDTH.

Fabric Length: Measure from your waist, to where you would like your skirt to end, and add 8cm/3 in.

Ribbon: 2x1 metre or approx. 2x1 yard lengths of ribbon to match your fabric, between 2, 3 or 4cm wide (3/4 to 1½ in.)

STEP 1
Measure yourself and cut your fabric according to the directions above. Iron your fabric until any creases are gone. With the WRONG side of the fabric facing up, fold each of the 2 short sides towards you, by 2cm/¾ in., iron to hold in place, then sew. Repeat to create a neat hem (see also Page 23).

STEP 2
Do the same with the 2 long edges of the fabric — these will be the waist and hem of your finished skirt. Turn towards you by 2cm/¾ in. iron, sew in place and repeat turn by 2cm/¾ in., iron, sew to make a neat hem.

STEP 3
For the waistband of the skirt, we now need to make a casing big enough to slip the ribbon into. What width is your ribbon? Add 2cm/¾in. to this number, and turn the top edge of your fabric towards you by this amount and iron. i.e if your ribbon is 3cm/1¼ in. wide, make your casing 5cm/2in. deep. Now sew this casing, making sure your stitches are close to the hemmed edge of the fabric (so that the finished casing is big enough to slip your ribbon into).

STEP 4
Take your 2 pieces of ribbon (1m/yd each) and sew a tiny hem at one end of each piece. Now tuck the raw edge of one piece of ribbon into one end of the casing, with about 3cm/1¼ in. of the ribbon right inside the casing. Now sew in place. Do the same with the other side. Now check for any stray pins before trying on your skirt. It's a Wrap!

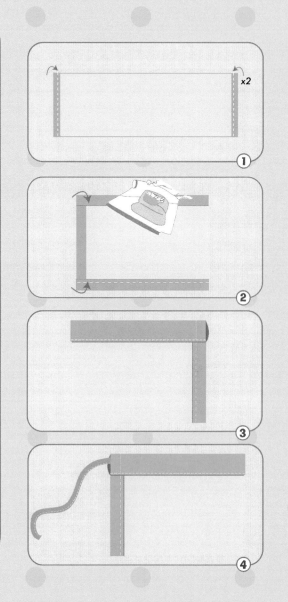

Make it! Bow Bag

Fabric 1: For the bag, cut 2 pieces of fabric, 30cm x 35cm/12 x 13¾in.
Fabric 2: For the handles, cut 2 pieces of fabric, 70cm x 10cm/27½ x 4in.
Fabric 2: For the bow, cut 2 pieces 110cm x 10cm/43 x 4in.

STEP 1
Hem the short edge of each piece of bag fabric.

STEP 2
To make the handles, fold each strip in half length-ways, right side facing in. Sew along the length, 2cm/¾ in. in from the edge. Turn tube inside out using a ruler or knitting needle. Iron flat, then stitch all around the outside edges of the handle, just in from the edge to neaten. Pin handles in place, 5cms/2 in. in from the edge of your bag, sew securely.

STEP 3
Place your bag fabric right sides together and pin. Sew from one top side to the other remembering to sew lock stitches at the start and finish. Now turn your bag the right way out!

STEP 4
To make the bow, pin the 2 lengths of fabric together and sew all the way around, leaving a 6cm/2.5 in. gap near the middle. Turn right side out,and sew up the gap. You can also either iron orsew all around the fabric length for a final finish. Now tie your bow around one of the handles to finish your bow bag.

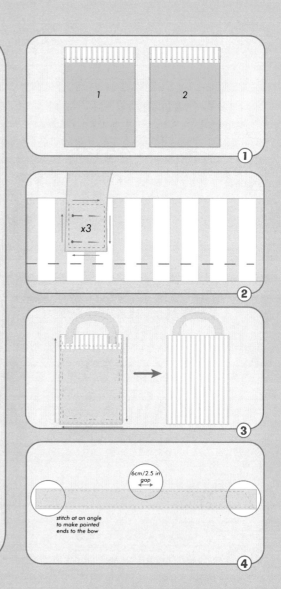

Make it! Shirt Dress/Top

Does your dad, grandfather or uncle have any old smart shirts they no longer need? Quick — grab them now, and in no time at all you could make yourself a brand new dress or tube top! Whether you will have enough shirt fabric for a dress or a top depends on a couple of things — the size of the shirt you begin with, and the size of the person it's for! Read through the steps and you'll soon see why! You will also need some elastic (2cm/¾in. width) and a ruler.

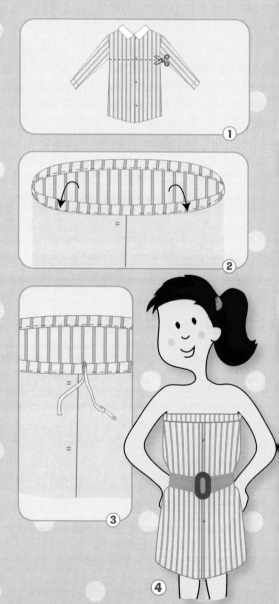

STEP 1
Iron the shirt so there are no wrinkles, and lay it out on a flat surface, buttoning it up and ensuring the front and the back of the shirt lay directly on top of each other with the bottom seams level. Use a ruler to mark a straight line from just under one arm across to the other side. Cut with sharp scissors.

STEP 2
Now you have a shirt "tube", so you need to make a casing at the top for the elastic which will hold your dress/top up. Turn the tube inside out, and turn the fabric by 1cm/½in. towards you. Iron this in place, pin, and carefully sew a hem all around the tube. Do this same again, this time turning the fabric by 3cm/1¼in. Iron, pin and sew — making sure your seam is close to the fabric edge so that there is room in the casing to insert your elastic! Stop sewing just before you get back to where you started.

STEP 3
Measure around the top of your chest, just under your armpits, and add 5cm/2in. Cut a piece of elastic to this size. Attach a safety pin to one end and use this to help you guide the elastic through the casing. When the elastic comes back out of the other end of the casing, use the safety pin to hold both ends together for now.

STEP 4
Turn right sides out and try your dress/top on. Adjust the elastic across the top of your chest until it feels comfortable — you will then pin and sew the elastic together to secure it. How does the length look — is it long enough to be a dress, with a lovely belt around your waist? Too short as a dress, or prefer it as a top? No problem — just mark where you want the bottom of your top to be, and add 2cm/3.4in.) Then simply follow the instructions on Page 23 to make a new hem.

T-shirt Skirt

Here's another great way to transform an old t-shirt or sweatshirt — this time into a cute little beach skirt! The bigger the tee that you use, the looser your skirt will be. An adult-sized t-shirt works well! Just make sure whatever shirt you use fits well over your hips and bottom!

You will also need: Cord or ribbon — double your waist measurement, and a large safety pin.

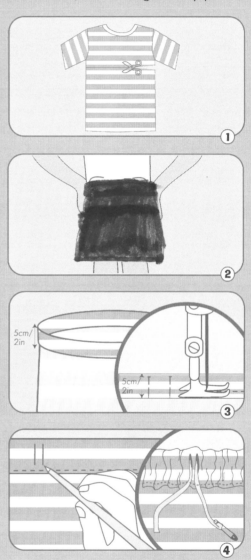

STEP 1
Lay your t-shirt evenly on a flat surface, making sure neither the back or the front are wrinkled. Use a ruler to mark a straight line from underneath one armpit to another. Now cut across this, cutting through both front and back of the t-shirt.

STEP 2
Turn the t-shirt tube inside out, and pull your "skirt" on. Turn the extra fabric at the waist over, until the bottom hem of the t shirt rests at the length you would like your finished skirt to be. Carefully pin in place and remove the "skirt".

STEP 3
Now we need to create a casing for the drawstring waistband. If the extra fabric you have turned over at the waist is more than 5cm, trim until only 5cm extra remains. With t-shirt still inside out, fold over 1cm/½in., iron in place, then turn again by 3cm\1¼in., iron and stitch in place, close to the bottom of the casing.

STEP 4
Now turn your skirt right sides out. In the centre of the front of your skirt, mark 2 slits in the casing, large enough for your drawstring or ribbon. Snip carefully with sharp scissors. Fasten a safety pin to one end of your card, thread the drawstring into the casing through one buttonhole and out the other end — pull until both ends are even and remove safety pin. Tie a knot in each end of drawstring. Now off to the beach you go!

 # **One Shoulder Top**

Transform an old t-shirt into a cool, one shoulder, summer top in just a few easy steps! You'll need an old t-shirt, a ruler and some dressmaker's chalk!

STEP 1

Lay your t shirt on a flat surface and lay your ruler diagonally across the front. One end should be just underneath the armpit, the other at the opposite side of the neck opening, just outside the neck seam. Mark the line with dressmaker's chalk, then cut along this line — cutting all the way through the front and back of the t-shirt at the same time.

STEP 2

Now cut off the other sleeve and cut across the shoulder seam.

STEP 3

Now tidy up the raw edges by hemming the new raw edges on the front and the back of your top. Turn your t-shirt inside out so the wrong side of the t shirt is facing you. Turn over the raw edge by 1cm/½in., iron and stitch in place. Repeat on the other side of t-shirt.

STEP 4

Turn back the correct way, and pull your top over your head, then tie in a knot at the shoulder.

Viola! You've just made a funky new top!

Inside of t-shirt

arvellous Mittens

...rself an old woolen sweater (a tightly woven wool knit or sweatshirt material works best
...ns) and give it a whole new lease of life as a cute pair of winter mittens. They're so easy to make,
and sure to come in….handy!!

STEP 1
First up we need to make a pattern! Place one hand
on a piece of paper and draw around the outline of
your hand — around 2cm/¾in. beyond your long-
est finger. Go all around your fingers then down and
around your thumb to create a mitten-shaped pattern.
Trace this to make a second pattern.

STEP 2
Place each mitten pattern so that the wrist edge of pattern your lines up with the waistband of the sweater
— this will give your mittens a stylish cuff! Pin in place
— making sure you are pinning through the pattern
AND the front and back layer of the sweater. Use a
sharp pair of scissors to cut around the mitten tem-
plates and through the sweater layers.

STEP 3
Remove the pins and the pattern. If you are planning
to decorate your mittens, do it now before you sew
them together, it will be much easier this way.

STEP 4
Now place two layers so that the RIGHT sides (the
outside of the original sweater) are facing in. Pin in
place. Sew from one side of the cuff, all around the
mitten edge (about 1cm/½in. in from the raw edge)
to the other side of the cuff. Don't forget to lock stitch
at the beginning or end or your stitches will burst!
Now repeat with the other mitten, turn right sides
out…and wear! How easy was that?

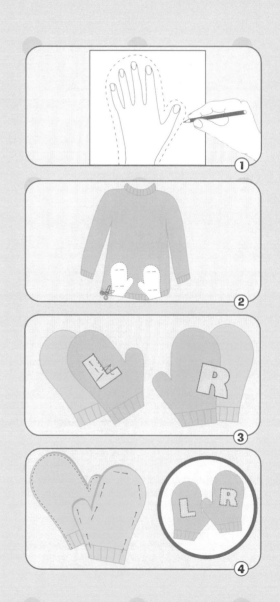

Jeans Skirt

If you have an old pair of jeans that are perhaps too short, or too worn at the knees, it's really easy to transform them into a cool denim skirt or mini. You can create a whole new look with very little effort! You will also need a seam ripper, and a funky fabric if desired.

STEP 1
Try on your jeans and make a mark on the leg, just below where you would like your new skirt to end. Lay them flat on a table and draw a line across both legs, level with the mark. Cut off the extra leg material and keep this as you may need it later. Use your seam ripper to open up the seams on the inside of the legs, and around the crotch of your jeans. On the front of your jeans, continue to open up the crotch seam to just below the zipper. On the back crotch seam, open up about another 7cm/3in.

STEP 2
Lay your skirt flat and pin down the overlapping flap at the front. Turn the skirt over and do the same with the flap at the back. Now sew these in place, following the line of the stitches that you had ripped out.

STEP 3
Now you need to fill in the triangular "gap" at the front and back to turn this into a proper skirt. Will you use the extra denim? Or a funky fabric? Turn your skirt so that the WRONG side is facing you, and carefully cut and pin a piece of fabric where the open space is. Turn skirt to the right side and carefully stitch the insert in place, being careful to take out pins as you go along.

STEP 4
Do the same with the insert on the back of the skirt. Then tidy up any extra fabric inside the skirt. Try your skirt on again and get a friend to help pin a hem in place at the desired length, then sew a simple hem or just leave a cool, frayed edge.

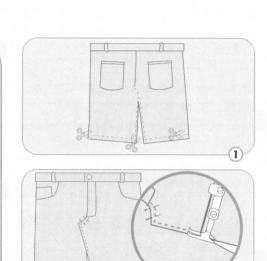

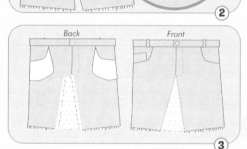

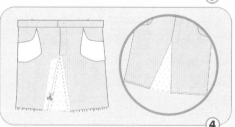

...ge Pants

...ke a "real" tissue sewing pattern, you can make your own simple pattern using a pair of your ...ns — this will help you get used to using patterns AND you can make a cool pair of comfy lounging ...nts too!

You will need: A large sheet of newspaper, parcel paper, or sheets of paper taped together.
A pair of jeans or pants in your size. 2.5m/2⅔ yds OR 1.5m/1⅔ yds of fabric (115cm/45 in. wide)
Elastic: 2cm/¾in. wide x the measurement around your waist plus 5cm/2in. added on.

STEP 1
Fold your pants in half by laying each leg on top of each other, and pulling the crotch area out. Place on top of the paper on a flat surface. Trace a line all around the pants, then draw another line 2.5cm/1in. all around the pants EXCEPT above the waistband where you need to draw a line 4cm/1½ in. away. Cut the paper pattern around the OUTSIDE lines.

STEP 2
Lay your fabric, right sides up, on a flat surface. Fold from the left until the folded section of the fabric is just slightly wider than your paper pattern. Lay the long, flat edge of your pattern along the fold in the fabric, and pin carefully in place, all around the pattern. Cut around the pattern through both layers of fabric. Now repeat with the remaining fabric — fold, position pattern, pin and cut.

STEP 3
Remove the pins and pattern and you will now have 2 identical pieces of fabric. With the RIGHT sides together, make sure the edges are all even, then pin from just below the crotch area to the bottom of the leg. Do this on both pieces.

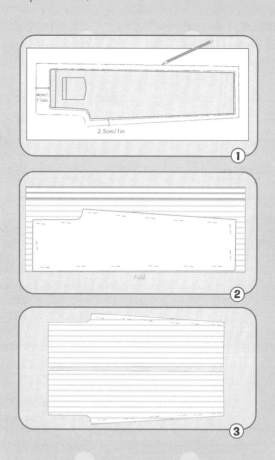

4cm/1½in

2.5cm/1in

①

Fold

②

③

STEP 4

Now stitch from under the crotch to the bottom of the leg — making sure your stitches are a straight line, and around 1cm/½in. from the raw edge. Remove the pins as you sew. You now have 2 "legs"!

STEP 5

Turn one of the legs RIGHT side out, then slide it inside the other leg so that the curves of the crotch area match up.

STEP 6

Now stitch this crotch seam, again with a 1cm/½in. seam allowance. Then repeat, sewing a second seam on top of the first one, to make your crotch seams stronger. Then pull the leg out of the other leg, but keep the pants inside out (so that the WRONG side of the fabric is on show).

STEP 7

Now it's time to make a casing for the waistband of your pants. First fold over 1cm/½in. to the wrong side and iron in place. Then fold over another 2.5cm/1in. iron and pin in place.

STEP 8

Starting off at the seam on one side, sew all around the casing, making sure your stitches are close to the bottom edge of the fabric (you need to leave enough of a "tunnel" in the casing for your elastic to fit through). Remove the pins as you sew. Sewing all around until you are almost, but not quite, back where you started stitching — finish about 2.5cm/1in. from where your stitches started.

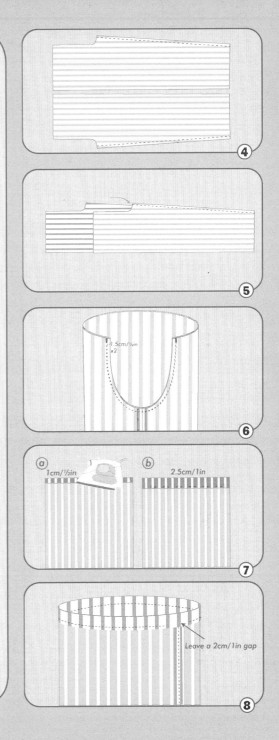

STEP 9

Measure around your waist and add 5cm/2in. and cut a piece of elastic to this size. Attach a safety pin to one end and use this to help you guide the elastic through the casing. When the elastic comes back out of the other end of the casing, use the safety pin to hold both ends together for now.

STEP 10

Try on your pants, and adjust the elastic until the waistband is comfortable. Secure with safety pin. Take off the pants and use your machine to stitch the elastic together, with a couple of overlapping seams for strength. Then stitch the opening closed.

STEP 11

Are your pants the correct length? Try them on again, outside in, and turn up a hem at your desired length. Trim the extra fabric until only 3.5cm/1½ in. remains. First fold over a 1cm/½ in. hem and iron in place. Then fold over by 2.5cm/1in. and iron and pin in place. Stitch all around, close to the inside egde. Now you have hemmed your pants. Check for any stray pins...put on your lounge pants ...aaaaand RELAX!

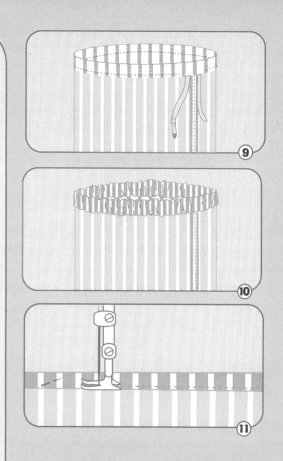

Top Tip!

You can make pants in lots of different sizes and styles — boxers, shorts, capris....a whole new closet-full of possibilities!

Learn to Sew: Kids

I hope you've had tons of fun learning to sew...why not add to your skills with my other books:

Learn To Sew: Kids
My First Hand Sewing Book

The perfect introduction to sewing for beginners. Follow Daisy Doublestitch and Billy Bobbin as they show you how to sew by hand and learn lots of easy stitches and sewing skills. Make super cool projects like Cupcake Pincushions, Crazy Creatures, Birdy Garlands, lovely Love Hearts and more!

Learn To Sew: Kids
Learn to Sew!

Learn how to sew with Daisy Doublestitch and Billy Bobbin, and make some super cool projects, including Kitten Slippers, Cute Cushions, Strawberry Purses, Tissue Monsters and more! Perfect for beginners!

Learn To Sew: Kids
My First Sewing Machine

Get started with your first sewing machine with easy to follow illustrations and instructions! Learn all the parts of a machine and what they do, how to thread your machine and wind your bobbin, how to start and stop sewing, turn corners... AND make your first easy projects — cushions, bags, zip cases, skirts, i-pod cases and more! Sew much fun!